39 Boys On Ground

Victor David Sandiego

39 Boys On Ground

To young adults and children who ran with abandon into the iron arms of hunger and war. Some returned and carried on, made their lives in the cities and on the farms. For the others, although you may be with ants in some forgotten field, many of us walk with you in spirit and may even call you by your true name as we sprinkle rice.

Contents

39 Boys On Ground

Introduction

Let him who seeks not cease to seek until he finds
And when he finds he will be troubled
When he has been troubled he will marvel

The Gospel According to Thomas

Daddy? Will you love me if I kill some boys for you? Put my finger on the trigger.

Will you forgive me for wrecking the Buick if I crawl on elbows and knees through the same jungle as you?

I lied about the baseball bat. You knew that. Put my finger on the trigger.

Daddy, please. I'll pull the pin on other sons rising from daddy shadow, running from daddy wrath, put my finger on the button, wired to explosive roads.

We are boys climbing from the hollows of our youth to manhood. We'll leave behind some speckled flags and low bugle notes for you, Daddy.

Telescope Power

1. Lunch Menu Is Missing

Look at me: a sack of weak and wobbly drought-dried skin and bones on the ground with my hands to the African wind.

I don't know another world but someday I hope to grow and show you I can think beyond my shrunken gut. I'll be an artist painting life with words or brushes – or maybe on a tyrant-rage with blood on the canvas of my kin.

The god I thought I knew is silent. I hear only an odd tune in my head: of Abraham, and how he took up the knife to carve his son into sacrifice.

How to please my muscles when I barely lift my head? Dry grass and buffalo dung don't cut it. I could count to three and clap my hands for magic bread to fall from sky but dust has made the magic dry – I think sky must first have rain.

I wonder: can you help me to regain the sense of worth I had before the hunger claimed me? I've had nothing to eat since they took my mother away.

2. Meanwhile, On The Other Side Of The World

Another boy plays with plastic toys. He crawls through grass with yard signs and popsicle sticks to look for funny food like worms or ants. His pants are blue and sturdy but time for new, he's getting fat.

I love this game, he says. Pretending to hunger. I'd rather be killing Cong like father in his war. But he's away for now, saving me from tyranny, and besides – I'm just a stripling.

If we came from monkeys with their funny hoots and howling like my science teacher says, then that would be my distant cousin on the television begging.

> But I don't care about his famine. It's time to purge and plunge my bowels! My supper starts again in 10 minutes!

* * *

Someday this boy will climb from the uninviting confines of his heart. His easy landscape of indifference may change.

Then he will say: Let me pause in each dead cornfield, touch each motionless boy – and call him by his true name as I sprinkle rice.

3. Reality Comes And Goes

Lately my life is but a mist in my sickness as I crawl through a curtain of grass to find a tree to scratch my back in the African barefoot dirt.

Looks like my stomach hasn't been so thriving, just a pinecone to offer it today. But far away, I believe at least I see another day coming.

In dream fever, I grew up and finally gripped my hands with the strength of strong bones. My father flickered there in song. He was spreading foe like dirt.

We ate sweet corn when rains washed our crops and we feasted on mutton and muffins.

But that was last night, before the blanket of darkness rotted. Still, I am thankful to chew a bit of barley. To dip my hands in a hole of muddy water, where the wild tongues of oxen often go.

4. I Could Run Antelope Down

I rise on my leg stumps far from my village, eye level with goats.

If I had goats.

The war stole them – when I could run antelope down.

My shoe size is gone.

If I had shoes.

I only need short pants and I have pants (thankfully) so I can beg with my legless clothes on for a wooden bowl of rice to go with my entrée.

If I had an entrée.

The rebels took them all away using my legs as stilts, leaving me stumps and 9 inch thigh bones. My former fast feet fastened to a tree. My alms? Rusty slugs of electrical conduit.

If I had a long time to make me rich, I swear I would build a new house with low windows.

5. Just Asking

Now I'm living on pebbles and beans. It's not so bad as it seems. Once in a while, a tourist bus stops. With maps and cameras and clocks in their hands, they try to view the skies through my eyes.

I ask, always real polite: Can you spare two shovels of dirt so I can climb from my pit? I'd like to see the stars, to laugh in the African light of the moon. I'd like to make my hunger the size of a shadow at noon.

When I see guns that never want for a round to fill their chambers, I start to think that people value dying. I start to wonder if my love for life is foolish and ill and how much better I would feel if I bound my heart in malice.

Please: when you go back to your land, after you nap and unpack, ask your Uncle Sam to help me. Tell him: I'll be on his firing squad. I'm ready to change the names of my gods.

6. For The Love Of Meat

Here I am covered in sniper dirt, my neck creased, my finger ready to help a stranger meet in peace with his maker.

I used to believe in cows and warm milk. For a while, I remembered girls, their smooth stone laughter, and how they drew me to the tall grass.

Now I'm just another boy on the ground, breathing with quiet fear. A man is moving below, the back of his wild head of hair exposed.

My god, my trigger needs love! Oh, squeeze me to cough it hard with message to bulls eye! Now run!! As fast as my legs can go into the bush.

My reward is deer meat and biscuit. I chew with an early moon on my shoulder and cry inside a little bit (where men don't hear) that my stomach is no more this night a sharp pointed stick in my gut.

7. This May Not Be What I Signed Up For

After the explosion, I am comfortable enough. Crumpled somewhat. My shirt torn. But alive.

Back to work I suppose handing out tickets to the crusade, but...

Where are my fingers to clutch and wiggle: *This is the church and the people!*

Where are my ears? I hear nothing but dull red ringing.

And what about my nose? It has left my face in search of better smells than me no doubt.

My eyes are merely closed, pretending to be blind. My neck still runs between my voice and my head.

8. On The Roadside

Let me through. I am minister from the east with my black-and-white belief in an honorable cause. Only moments have passed, my walkie-talkie squawking, since my son fell.

He is everything I own since my home was repossessed. He swims to me crying soft of metal fingers in his throat. He touches my face, shaving me with looks, my magnificent son.

He gropes for my knee, gargles a little marching song, calls me Papa.

Let me put a hand on his chest. Please. Let me start his heart pump up and I promise: to cease my frantic longing for another war.

9. There Is Value In The Dreamer

Oh, I love to sit on stone and dream of days far away from this spell of slow hours when I can run the lion down and sleep on his blanket!

It's always fun to think of other worlds and other ways of living. To think of how the tower of my life could rumble and rise until I stand on clouds far above this quiet rock.

That's right. I dream to have a bigger, better life. And if you don't agree with me, raise your toe! I will step on it!

I don't want to burn huts. I don't want to kill my brother. I'd love to have a telescope, and from this scrap of soil where we huddle, share that patch of rapture in the heavens with my kin.

We *can* infect the brutal beasts of our instincts with compassion – and rise above the smell of swine that roam the countryside in jeeps. We *can* bring our families to the same table and feast.

10. Now Back To My Journey

Please hold the train. I am on the track, downwind from the station. I would welcome it if you would not cut off my other leg.

Only a little tired, otherwise well. A rusty rest for my leg stump gives me a bit of a boost. Thank you. You are most kind to allow me to have my breather.

I'd like to get wherever I'm going faster, but a ticket on your train is out of reach for me. My sack of belongings washed away at the last crossing.

11. Before The Fighting Broke Out

My father stoops down to carry me on his big bushy neck. I'm faster than the landscape now, and much taller, too!

Remember rocks and hard knocks? No. I haven't even learned them yet!

There's always a snack nearby, I never weep hunger. Snake likes me to caress him. Bird urges me with warbles to gently comb his wing.

I suppose in time, pavement might erode my flesh as I'm dragged down the road by a truck. But that just sounds like bad luck blues or the outcast past wanting back.

12. The Lion Must Also Eat

There is no map wrapped in my mind for my trail as I slap mosquito with my tail. I swish your scent up, flip it around my whiskers into my nose:

Ah, BOY MEAT! For my teeth. A couple of valleys over. It might take some time, but boy meat is sublime and once I catch a whiff, I do not let go.

After I run him into the ground, I drag him into the shade and consummate my craving. I can eat but once a week when I chow down on boy meat.

13. God Might Have A Sense Of Justice After All

From my tall perch (some say, beyond the sky), I see a boy on the ground next to a flock of sheep. He's sleeping in the sun. A green and narrow field on an easy slope.

I cherish the touch of his life as he grows slow to a man, beneath my hand. His desires to run through the pale breath of dawn, to have friendship and love, must not be ripped from his heart.

Since I foresee everything, permit me to reveal: One day his leg will be seized and severed – and he will let it leave him. Instead of wails and retribution, his compassion will grow.

Yes, even man – who I fashioned from clay into the doppelgänger of imperfection – can climb from the naked lowland of his instinct and paint the world a brighter shade of grass stained green.

First Intermission

Well, that's thirteen steps and thirteen sacks of sad stories, a raw and radiant prime number, the count of gallows planks or cookies in a baker's dozen.

I know it's hard to see humor in injustice and pain when the symphonies of pleasures we attend sometimes only seem to help us make it through the day without crying.

But follow me further before you give up on finding something funny. Quite a few of my boys float with their face *up* in the bathtub – and still smell like warm honey.

In Search Of Gorgandú

14. The Real Conflict Begins

Are you still here? Want me to go away? Perhaps I'll outlast the embarrassed fabrication you texture with such astonishing clarity when you declare my existence acceptable.

Do you ask my name yet? You sprinkle rice? That makes it my own. My finger leaves the trigger alone.

I wash my foot in the river, forget all my friends, all the boys I left behind. Soon though, their voices will catch me, wrap my neck in colorful ropes.

But what else can I hope to do? I must stampede a village for food.

And yet I choke up badly when I put my ear on the open ground – for from this twisted place, I hear flowers growing from my weeping father's face.

15. How We Sacrifice Our Youth

This can't be good: They're dragging me to the altar by my hair and I hear the ritual whetstones as they greet the long knives.

WAIT. I am only 10 years old. I can't make the crops grow.

I haven't kissed a girl yet. Haven't swam in the cool river one more time.

I could run away into the jungle if they would stop stretching my neck. Become a hermit boy, live on bugs. And when they've given up – forgotten why they want to sprinkle my blood on the ground – sneak back after crickets sleep, lie down with my mother.

Can't you see? Surely an old man of fifty winters has richer bone marrow than me?

16. The Suburban Privilege Of A Steady Diet

With her *come-to-supper* voice, my mother calls me in, but there's a thousand ants on my arm up to the rubber band where my boy bicep is still thin. And no, they don't nibble on my skin. They only tickle like a light ripple of pins.

Now mother calls with her *milk-the-cow inflection*, but that's only a private joke between us, a sign of our affection.

An early evening searchlight marks a far parking lot, sweeps me back and forth. How I love to climb these lovely shafts of light high into the sky and from there see the city wrapped in supermarkets.

One day the power went out and we couldn't have popcorn with our butter. It still makes me queasy or even ill to recall how we hunkered down with candles and howled.

But back to my ants! They clap their tiny mandibles! Then slide down the light on rafts of green leaves to make me giggle and snort.

Now mother calls me with her *pot roast* voice, one I can never ignore. But that's okay, it's in agreement with my lips. I run for the comfort of the kitchen – and just for fun, try on a sense of hopeless hunger. To see how it looks on my face. Like war paint, when the distant drums of unfed thunder rumble.

17. We've Got Your Back, Son

Think of it as stiffening your spine, or making your father proud. He endowed you with the gift of his name and you wouldn't want to shame him, or make him weep without a flag if you got killed in a lousy street gang.

But you cannot speak of the bonus we drop from the sky onto peasants in far away lands. That's enough to frag you. That'll just drag your reputation into the dirt with the Leavenworth bums.

Look, streetwise or book smart, we've got your back. So open your arms to our troop strength. It's the macho thing to do for any kid who needs to grow up fast, leave his teenage angst in the gutter.

And you will be the envy of all of your useless friends who stayed behind, those who permit the country to slide into defenseless darkness.

Remember: we'll help you learn a secret trade – and should you break your bat during the interrogation, we'll drag the whimpering scumbag away by his armpit for you.

Now sign: boots and boys on the ground in 17 hours. It's time you paid your country back, son. It's time to wager the balance of your years.

18. Always Look On The Bright Side Of Life

To crawl in dirt is good for me – it stops illiterate rebels from reading my position. Oh, sometimes I just say: *the other side* (so I don't need a deck of cards) or if I am feeling windy, I pronounce them: *sons of god damn bitches*.

In my baby backyard dirt, I crawled to be alive instead of crawling to stay alive. In my baby boy mouth, I wanted to put the whole taste of each and every thing.

Oh sure, insurgents hold the street now but when I get through, I will find the rumored bakery of fresh cream! I plan to edge through the front door in anticipation, and then roll to the left real quick.

I'll rest my automatic rifle on the dairy case, lick my fingers for a while.

19. When You Don't Feel Like Getting Out Of Your Ditch

I want to live beyond this age of speeches. I want to make it past my prime. I want to be home with my friends on a porch of smokes and beer cans where – between the puffs and effervescent swallows – we can scoff at other boys, who boarded military buses, who didn't read between the lines of glory when the country marched another war across the headlines.

I'd like to see my father, too. Feel his hand on my shoulder, feel his fingers flex. I don't believe I ever told him that I care.

God, when I'm scattered on the verge of ruin, my hands I thought to be my friends betray me, become my shaking foe. I'd like to throw myself away from here, go back to the river where we tramped along the tender banks and coaxed the fish to eat the breaded hooks.

So don't order me to leap from my hiding place, please. To charge the gas. Don't tell me to bust my hollow flask of courage open.

20. The Hard Way, On A Hideous Hillside Of Coffins

I was caught up in the fad of flags, and maddened for reprisal. I shrieked and shouted. My sons answered the call. With jack-knife care, they took their fight to the target of our righteous rage.

But Missouri spring turns to fall when summer comes home in a box.

Hot ashes in my hair, a mouthful of crucifixion nails, thorns in my eyes.

All are welcome. If I could receive again, before the blood fever took me in, the gift of my boys as a treasure that could never be exchanged.

21. Who Is The Lucky One Now?

Put out hat with holes (but won't leak copper coin) for real good maybe
nickels buy some cat food or dim bag of 1st-Ave-don't-give-fuck-for-
you-Jack relief.

Maintain joyful hope amid bladder blues and homespun kindness from
cops: they only turn water cannons on in July.

But you in business suit need play catch up with misers and mask
uneasy truth: I am invisible to you, sound proof. Twenty times a week I
call you Mister when you walk on by in silence.

Evening, move to boxes and freeway caves, put my head on paper bag,
remember: those who at least nodded as if to sprinkle rice from their
hat instead of rushing past a ghost when I spoke.

22. After The Generals Finally Let Me Go

Now I am a mountain boy, free to amble through the pines. Free to cook my rice or eat it raw, to curse the underwriters of war and waltz to the evening sonatas of birds.

To hell with roads, I live on trickles and struggle to regain my mercy. It's never nice-and-tidy easy. And it might seem strange. But if you say human nature cannot change, you admit your powerlessness.

23. On The Way To Gorgandú

Somehow I need to find again the places where I went to wonder if I could forge a passage through my frozen years. These were slopes of summer mountains with their tumbled broken heaps of granite gods to climb upon and thrust me through the gate of heaven.

I was just a boy, the outcast youngest dreamer from a den of doers. My ambition was to flutter my wings.

Incoming bombastic attack from the commander way back in the bunker! And how I longed to climb the outer fence for him and bear his bruising hunger to slaughter yet another nation of boys.

Forgive me, I suffer from my past. At times, it gives me gas. But I believe that from this woodland where I trundle, with my lonesome dreadful days of living with my father's fury passed, I can empty, with a dash of salty grief, the pot of lethal soup we cooked in concert, as we battled and bartered for our place in the world of love.

24. How His Footsteps Echo

I think it was the entrance to his eyes he guarded jealously, behind the shuttered windows of his blindness. I think he hoarded admiration for his accidental son and only rolled it from his reticence when winter drowned beneath the summer lakes.

And so his eyes would drive me – with their sockets leaking light around the edges of his silence – into honest acts I tried to do to please him.

And on the day I caught the bus to start my killing bender, he stretched his hand across the nation, wished me a bullet full of luck, and urged me to heed the foreign coffins run amok among the spangled fields of fallen flowers.

I thought I could devour his wisdom, slurp it raw and dripping from the plate he held aloft. Those splendid skills he hammered with spikes. His talent for striking like a spear with words. That sense of power he conferred upon himself each time he rose to his shocking rightful height and like a preacher said: Only an irresponsible coward of biblical dimension seeks to fabricate a fence on the border of his blame.

25. White Water Flashback

With the help of highways, I floated across the continent to the San Joaquin and listened there on the banks as it counted its stories with pebbles and rocks to rapidly say that: even though I am a mighty river and can easily flood you with broken boats and death by drowning, know that I don't mean to ruin your Winston cartons or thrust your backpack to the lower fishing hole. I am an ancient ancestor of the mountain and my only rushing purpose is to mate with the sea. If you find yourself on an elephant rock in the middle of my journey, in the middle of the night, stranded amid the rapids, try to sleep a black rainbow. Tomorrow the sun will pierce the canyon and in the sharp whitewater light, you may try your luck to save your shoes and skin as you swim through my incurable current for shore.

26. Sometimes, It Really Is Magic

Take the dark heart of Conrad, I will lick it with salt all the way back to the headwaters for information foreign to me of an eminent chieftain way out in the bush.

I find him at last with snakes in his hat. He greets me in his caterpillar voice of drums. We feast on deer meat and onion leaves. He knows the word for living in 39 languages.

Water buffalo credits roll – bass voice beckons.

My eastern face to the sunrise, my primitive potential taller, I discover: It really is magic to grow flowers by waving your hand.

27. Awakening

Once more, my heart is buried in my wonderful womb, the one I knew before I arrived in this world of madness.

But I should climb the banks of the birth canal and see for myself if wisdom is but cold comfort and if buoyant days and astonishing candled nights can lift the latch of my love and heal or merely conceal my lesions and sores.

28. Through The Sleepless Night

Yet all I can do these last few nights is wait outside my cave for my body to come home. I must blindly wander in search of better thoughts than those that have camped like Gypsies on the threshold of morning. I haven't forgotten my ants. I still love them as I did before the hungry war. They trust me to crawl in the palms of my hands where I could crush them like an evil god.

With astonishing frequency, an eagle I have gently friended lands on my shoulder. He tattoos blood stigmata on my wrists and forearms. I don't mind. It only hurts until I close my eyes and visualize a world: where all may hunt their peaceful needs by day and spend their nights dreaming.

Doesn't make sense.

Things we do to our children

to ourselves.

When I finally leave the forest of my life behind, I hope to see the land beyond in bloom. The persevering age of monarchs has passed. At last we can stand, free by our own graces, a long abundant promise fulfilled.

Second Intermission

No need to trust my motives, but stay a while longer. Until the last human hand of dawn leaves its print on our door.

If I fail to make it from the building when the gods burst in, please attend to my last eleven children. Roll the taste of my boys over your tongue, and like tobacco leaves – help them greet with dignity this final aromatic act of flame.

Elephant Shadow

29. Soaring Scent Of Angels

Look at me: My face is full of tin. More than scraps of meat, I need faith to defeat my hunger. My smelly fingers, stubs of clay, are as they were the day I left the oven of my mother's womb and stood outside the world consumed by wonder.

See the image that is painted in my eyes. It's glorious to face the mirror alone and know that you have crumbled from the cradle of your birth back into the haven of our earth and from there climb a sky of dusty wind to blow the dirt and deeds that covered you in other lives away.

It's time for feet to trample on the dust of my bones, to appreciate the kindred spittle that flowed from the spigot of my father's rage, but let him leave this stage of life a better place alone.

My days are throwing rocks at me, my past and I must come to blows. For now, only my eyes see into this crystal coming phase. But from the coffin of my chest, my heart beats the wooden earth with bloody drums.

30. Fallen Flower

Cut him down – the hammer of his heart has ceased. Put him on the ground. I will wash his face with grief and search the rubble of the streets to find the thief that ripped his life away.

Cover those wounds with cloth. They leave only a trail of torment and discharge his dignity. Open your funeral mouth and feast on his words. We have a chance to rid the world of hate.

Later I will find the time to sleep it off. But now, hoist him on the scaffold of my shoulders and spine. Let me be his shrine. I will carry him to his grave like a cross.

31. When You're Tired Of Making Crime

So I'm waiting for my execution with a nod to the justice of my condition. I did steal a loaf just for fun to see the baker douse his dour face with sweat when he ran after me.

It's not that I'm broke. I'm just tired of living and now I can leave it to the prefect to decide my fate.

But I believe in resurrection, in the holy rendering that paints us all on a new canvas when the old one fades, is made obsolete by age, or is slashed by the knife into a thousand prism pieces in a lover's jealous rage.

Before I go, I'd like to say: Watch for me in elephant shadow! Hear me creaking under moon rise! I have friends on the other side: the boys I knew before we grew out of our younger pants into the world of just causes, my father who taught me to answer for my crime.

I'll turn my eye upward now and watch the rope drop. Today belongs to my throat to burn and break the copper coated notes. But tomorrow belongs to my new golden voice of celebration.

32. The Master Of War Must Die

Sometimes when I raise my arm on the first step of morning, the goblet of darkness shatters. It's as if I yet stood in defense of the light.

This day when I warm the bricks, I know he must be crucified. Nothing else will do. I must put my hands on his hammers, my feet on his spikes.

When the ground is gray with ash from the day we left him burning on the hill, maybe the soup lines will shorten. Maybe the armies of glut and greed let loose to swarm the locust land will shrivel.

I for one will bring my knife to his body on the altar. I will pay my respects with blood. My life is not a catacomb to fill with bony whispers. My heart is not a shopping cart to fill with day old bread.

33. Between The Helper And Helped

See that boy, his mouth is full of chains. Each time he puts a savior on his spoon, he spits. The favorite foot of his grandfather slithers past, on its way to Gorgandú, to protect this boy's freedom to live the way he chooses.

You would think this boy would not abuse his life, that he wouldn't run the streets with gangs of demons. That he would refuse to sink himself with stones of gloom into a lake of sorrow.

But consider that his want is warm and thrusting to his legs to find a place beneath a silent dripping tree of apple buds instead of winter rain to call his own. Consider that his home is cold, his father in the grave, his mother waving from a prostituted corner of the room to shut the door.

Now there is more to the cardboard cutout of his life than greets the jaundiced eye. This boy may be looking for answers to riddles: Who runs to Sampson's door with tigers? He may be looking to the heavens for bread. It's not for me to say which devils he needs to walk away from or which he should beat with iron bars until they moan. But I can help. I know a mountain lake. We'll kneel upon its morning shore – and rinse the troubles from our eyes with sunrise.

34. Marker Found On A Stone

When intrepid gods created me

before I arrived in this ground

I knew nothing.

Nothing is changed.

35. The Origin Of Our Memory

It is as if we came from the same river, you and I, and washed up upon the shore of open spaces. There we found a child growing from our arms that we wrapped around the earth and each other – and with him, discovered how to brush the dusty angels onto our faces.

Recall the boy we birthed filled the open ground with acres of saviors and split the green and blue bowels of the sky into two parts: one to enclose the limbs of all the children who fell beneath the wheels of war and the other to reflect into the blind topaz eyes of the world their illuminating and insistent innocence.

36. Crossing The Rivers That Run With Weeps And Wails

Well before that time though, the same boy toyed with devils. He was not a man when he called them to his shadowed room to walk the walls with spider legs. With the fluency of innocent ignorance, he coaxed them closer to the rope that stretched across his neck. And thus he built the layers of his strength up one by one and learned to repel the caustic ills of his poor world.

If you heard him curse and wail as he beat his demons back with bags of rags, you would think his struggle to climb into the arms of angels was lost, that he need only stumble once on a patch of spoiled ground to fall into a pit of skulls.

But now he knew his rivals and the tricks they played with evening light to make it seem like morning. He grew strong and consigned himself to the left hand of miracles, those that wake the heart from its slumber with a whisper rather than a shout. His allegiance came forth to stand for all to see on the rooftop of the midday sun. And from there he pledged with mouth spilling light and sky that one day the manner of his execution would be revealed.

37. The Day Our Friend Left For Gorgandú

Now dearly and with visible pain reflected from the river of my face, I recall the day my friend rode to my hillside on his horse, dismounted from the mountain of that beast, and stood there weeping.

He had come to die among the crosses, to feed the sky with his last wishes, his last – and ultimately his only – desire that man reunite with candles in the passages of peace.

And with him, he dragged his doubts and his fear that his sacrifice would be in vain. That the earth would spit out his bones. That a turbulent season of rain would wash his name away.

On that day I learned to trust the truth that ran like lions freed of ferocity from his mouth. As a boy, I put him down on the ground. I lit but one torch and clanged my hammer on the iron earth. The people came and stood in silence as I marked this place with pointed sticks, and covered them with cloth. And as he rose slowly with the wind, the knives in our throats withdrew. We watched as he shrank from our sight and disappeared, our hearts gray on the shelf of his shoulders and throbbing.

38. Message From The Troubled Water

At the tribunal, I stand as a mountain unmoving above the pale shadowed valley of my boyhood. Rain falls into the canyons of my eyes when the judges cast their ballots with stones. But my stream of tears flows over the ground to the river, carries off the paper scent of my ghost, and evaporates on the newborn banks of the day when the sun turns the water blue.

My days of finger and flame like the train are click-clacking. This must be the marvelous vision I saw from the red lips of the crater. This must be the field where the amputated legs go.

The boys I knew are here, their endless wars and famines as ants beneath their feet. No one person may pass our coffin from hand to hand. We have committed our bodies and our prescriptive beliefs directly to the earth.

I would not be so crude or cruel to ask that you follow me. The sky is full of hooks. But we are not meat in the butcher shop of god, and I will leave the cleavers on the chopping block. I will paint the world a brighter shade of faithful green along the sidewalks and lakeshores.

39. The Slow Path Of Our Longing

And when the soldiers bind the boy at last a man to the beams and drag the short body of his years over the ground to save their worthless conceit, my meager concerns lay severed and forgotten. Nothing can compare. I declare each piece of flawed love I chewed stiff and senseless. And if I light a prayer with candle flame, he may heal me.

From a magnificent distance, great in its ability to mask my imperfections, the craters from which I clambered are but hollows of the youthful earth where boys are birthed to ascend into a telescope and visit the sky. These are stories that came to me on knees and from the sweet scraping branches of the trees I trusted – and from the discarded leaves that floated to my foot when I stood on the autumn banks of rivers.

I have no voice to tell you to trust or deny the swollen hope I have that mankind can learn from its failings, can elevate its hunger. One by one, we learn to melt the bullets and arms. From the first boy crying on the ground to the last man alive on a hillside of crosses, we follow the slow path of our longing.

Afterword

I wrote *39 Boys on Ground* in 25 days, between May 5 and May 30, 2007. I didn't plan to write it at first. It was only after I had written the first piece that I thought I had discovered a thread that I must pull further. I didn't know what I was going to write about exactly but I did decide at the beginning on the number 39.

For me, 39 is a magical and symbolic number that appeals to my mathematical and philosophical sides. First, it is odd which gives it special significance. Even numbers represent rationality and reason as they can be divided into identical integer chunks, while odd numbers represent spirituality, realms and thinking that falls between cracks, and that which is less amenable to categorization. The number 39 contains an interesting relationship between prime numbers; it is the product of two primes (3 and 13) that each represent opposite end of human superstition, that is: 3 is considered lucky, 13 unlucky. Lastly, 39 has historical and allegorical significance as the number of stripes (or lashes) that were administered to Jesus.

I wanted very much to write *39 Boys on Ground* in one rapid push, a sort of organic orgasmic thrust of energy and ideas. I didn't want to drag it out. In many ways, it has been writing itself inside me for years and my desire and/or need was to stay as focused as I possibly could and get it written.

Of course, know too that even though I wrote the original manuscript quickly with a concentrated thrust of energy, I've been revisiting the words and revising them for a long time, almost endlessly it seems. It's the blessing and the curse of all authors who both love and struggle with their worlds and creations: the desire to attain a level of perfection which might qualify us for a sort of insane sainthood – or at least allow us to be considered a good parent to our children.

At any rate, as I write these words now in late 2012, I know that it's time to put my boys out in the world, missing limbs and all, and let them find other hearts to visit. My hope is that their viewpoints and experiences can help others – as they have done for me – encounter more of the world's beautiful complexity and variety, and appreciate how people from all corners of the globe have so much in common.

Victor David Sandiego

About The Pentology

In the spring of 2007, I wrote the two pieces which begin this volume. Although I didn't know it at the time, those two turned out to be the beginning of a multi-year effort to create an overarching five volume set of work.

These five volumes explore and commemorate a journey that begins with physical depravation in Africa and continues in an expanding sphere that passes through modern life in the Americas into a reawakened mysticism. In many ways, the journey is my own, but the stories are told from a wide variety of perspectives and circumstance.

The volumes in the pentology are: *39 Boys on Ground, 51 Men On Hills for Ships, 57 Women of the Earth, The 69 Names of God,* and *The 87 Faces of Creation.*

Sneak Preview

The following two pieces are from other series that I've written. The manuscripts as a whole haven't yet been published, but some of the individual pieces have been published in various magazines and journals.

The first piece is from *The First Book of Muwadi* and the second piece is from *The Second Book of Muwadi*.

Muwadi In Captivity

From the corner of the room:

An impatient man comes to me with news. The words leap from his mouth like mad barbarians. His chest convulses and twists sideways with the report of your capture.

The Capitán knows my face from the House of Friends; he unbolts the door, escorts me to your cell, withdraws.

Thirty six years ago:

I left your carrion to the crow, watched them circle and descend, watched them cluster and haggle over your flesh.

No mistake or error in judgment brings me to this place. Before I rolled you down the slope, you raised your lips to kiss my ear with the promise that we would meet again.

The voices:

from the street carry heavy timbers; the sky turns dark with their demands. Looking out, I see myself younger and more eager to condemn.

A lion obeys himself when his teeth take the prey. On that same hunt, I drove a whip with fierce madness and gnashed all who stood in my path.

In this moment:

You sit on a stone floor (you are always a stone), your eyes stationary and your mouth at rest.

My voice is a single gnat; you brush it aside in an imprecise arc of your forefinger.

Gratitude

When my death melted away and its mortal sickness passed, men and women became translucent again and once more I could see the color of their hearts. They bore their heaving breath in bushels as they rolled boulders aside to call on me in my tomb.

"We have forgotten your face," one of them cried and another said "No, it is your name that eludes us."

If I could, I would have spoken and advised them to look no farther than their own heart where all the truthful bits and pieces of God dwell, as a single rabbit though chopped and sliced, inhabits the stew.

But my throat was a cactus, as it is after every bout of death, and I thirsted for a lake of wine. The people saw my need and fetched a bowl of blood to wash the spines away.

Replenished, I dribbled thanks on my shirt and broke a bubble on my lips. "It is I who have forgotten," I managed to utter. "When ill, I see only devils; when in health, even the snakes are saints."

About The Author

Victor David Sandiego lives in the high desert of central México where he walks the cities and mountains, plays drums with jazz combos and in musical / poetry collaborations, writes, and studies. His work appears in various journals and on public radio.

For more information, see:

victordavid.com

www.ingramcontent.com/pod-product-compliance
Lightning Source LLC
Chambersburg PA
CBHW071637040426
42452CB00009B/1668